Drawn to Garden
Coloring Book

Illustrations by Erin Lau

Coloring Tips:

- Markers, Colored Pencils, Crayons and Oil Pastels will all work beautifully, but you are advised to add a blank sheet of paper under each page in case the colors bleed through.

- Be loose with your coloring if you can! Add shading, texture and changes in gradient to enhance the sense of depth.

- Try out different shades of green to create a sense of layering, as well as other foliage colors such as burgundy, gray, silver, and yellow. This will be especially useful for certain drawings that are zoomed out farther, and flowers are harder to see.

- Have fun!

for more visit:
drawntogarden.com

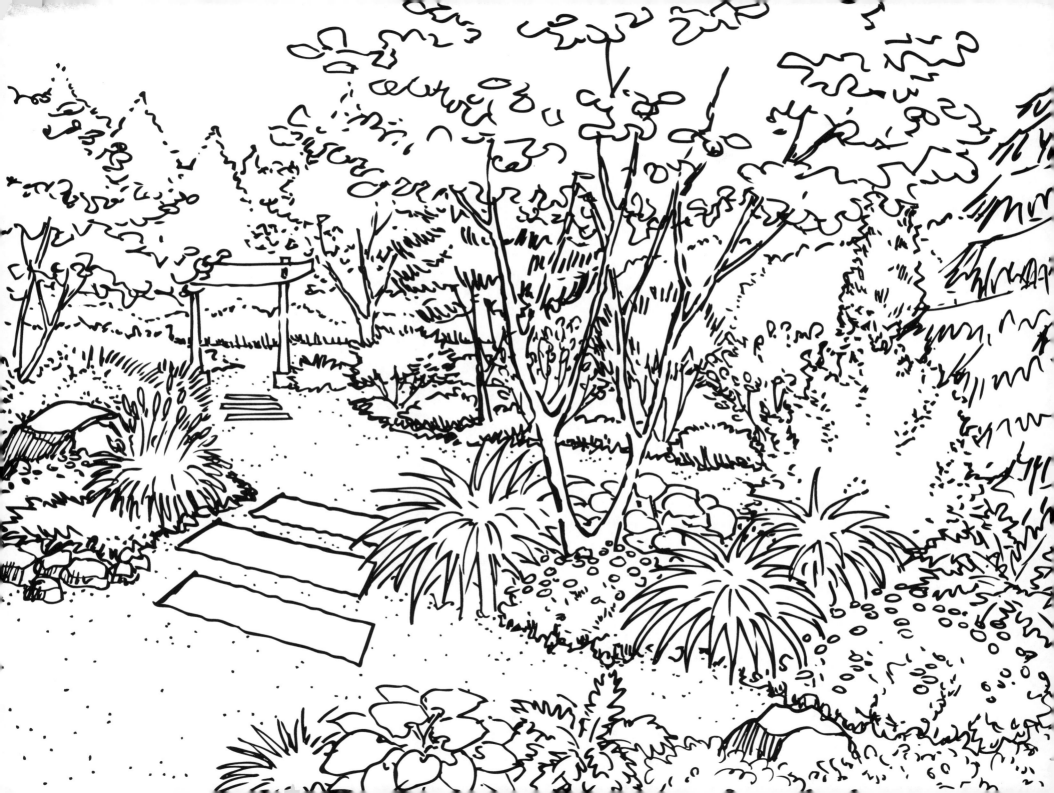

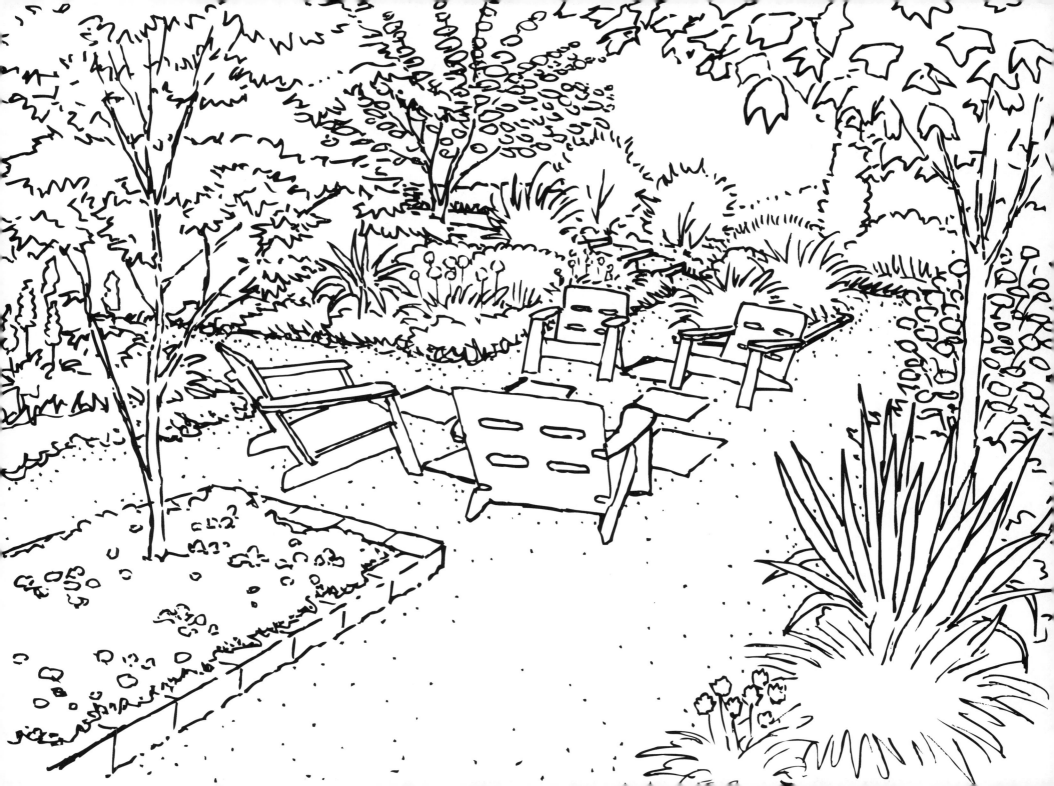

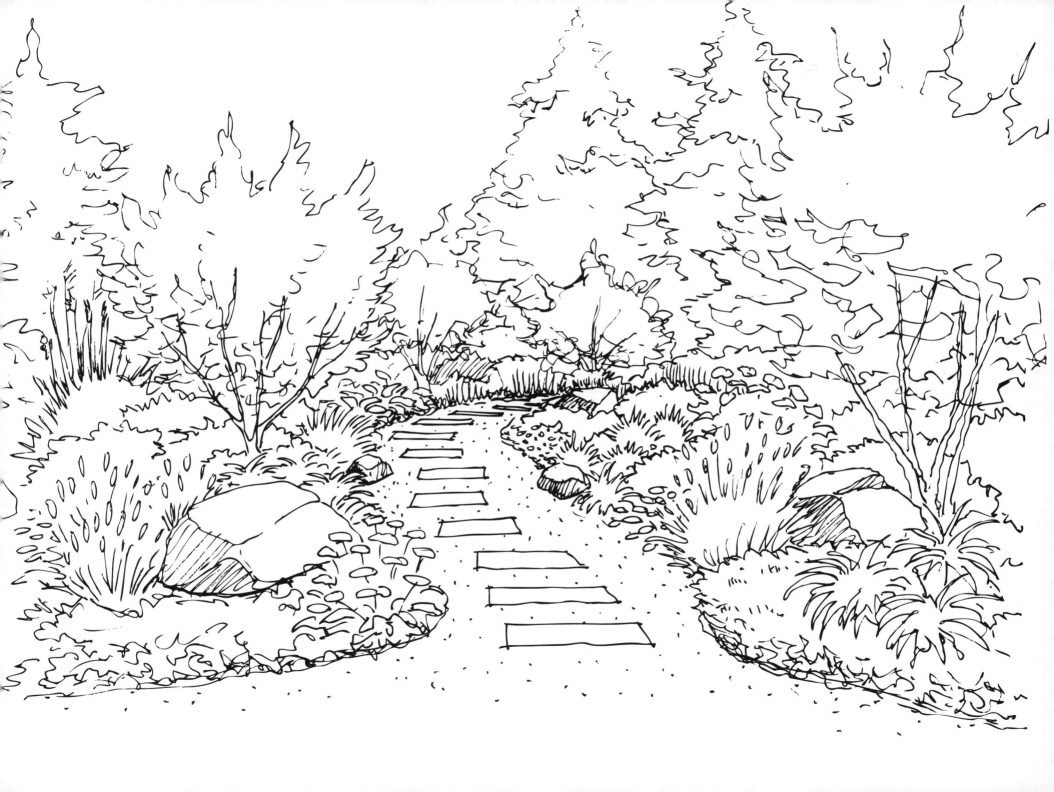

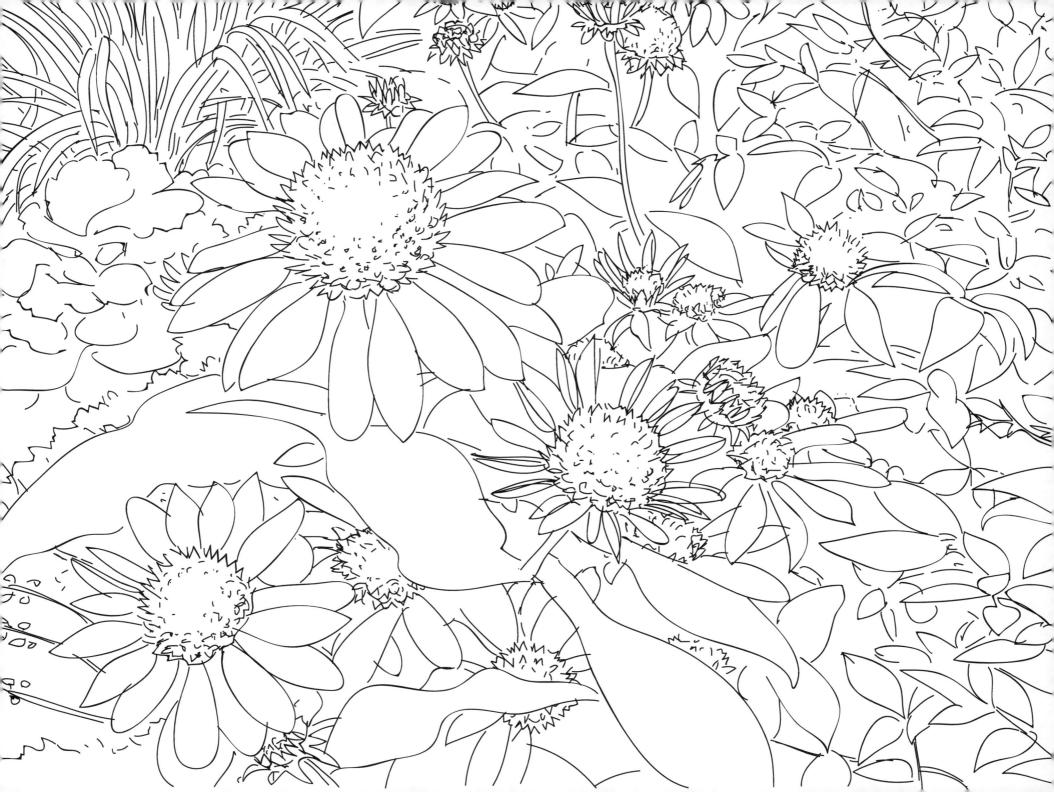

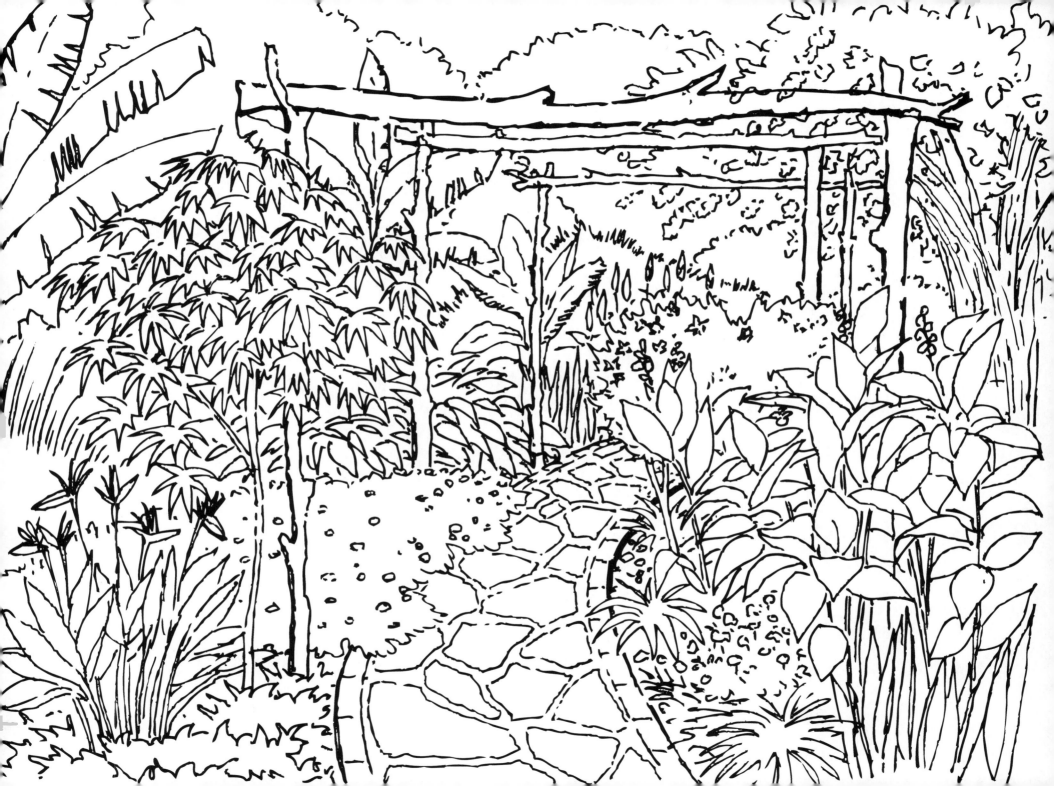

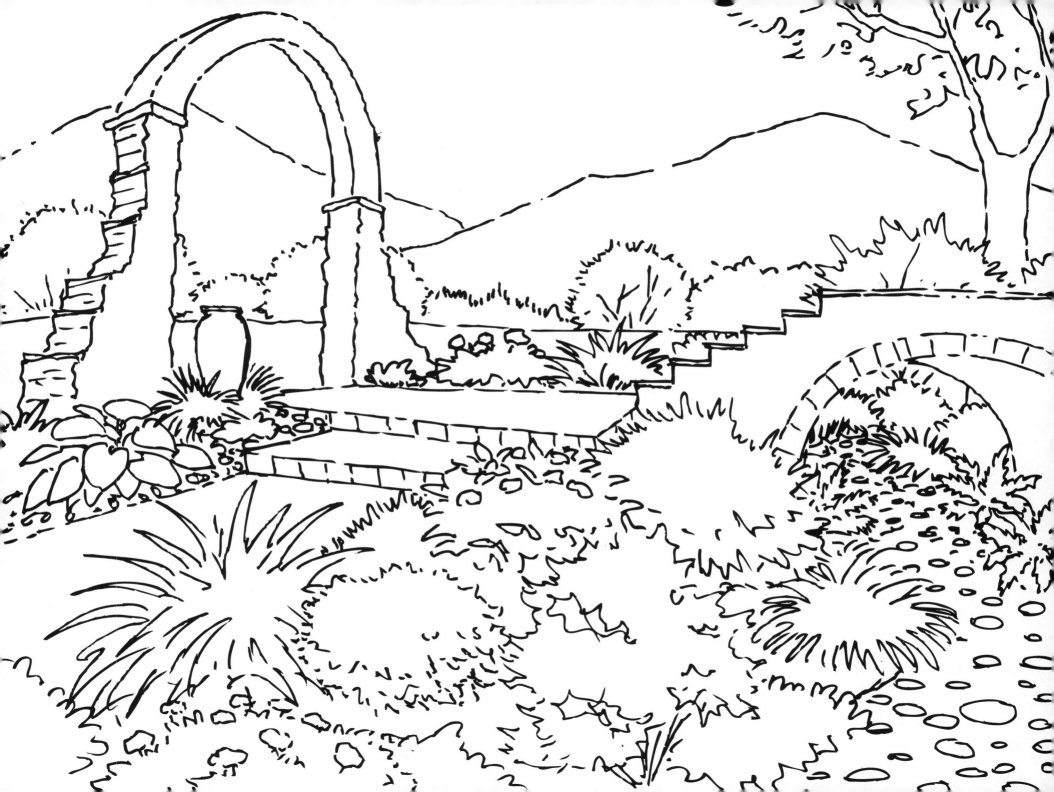

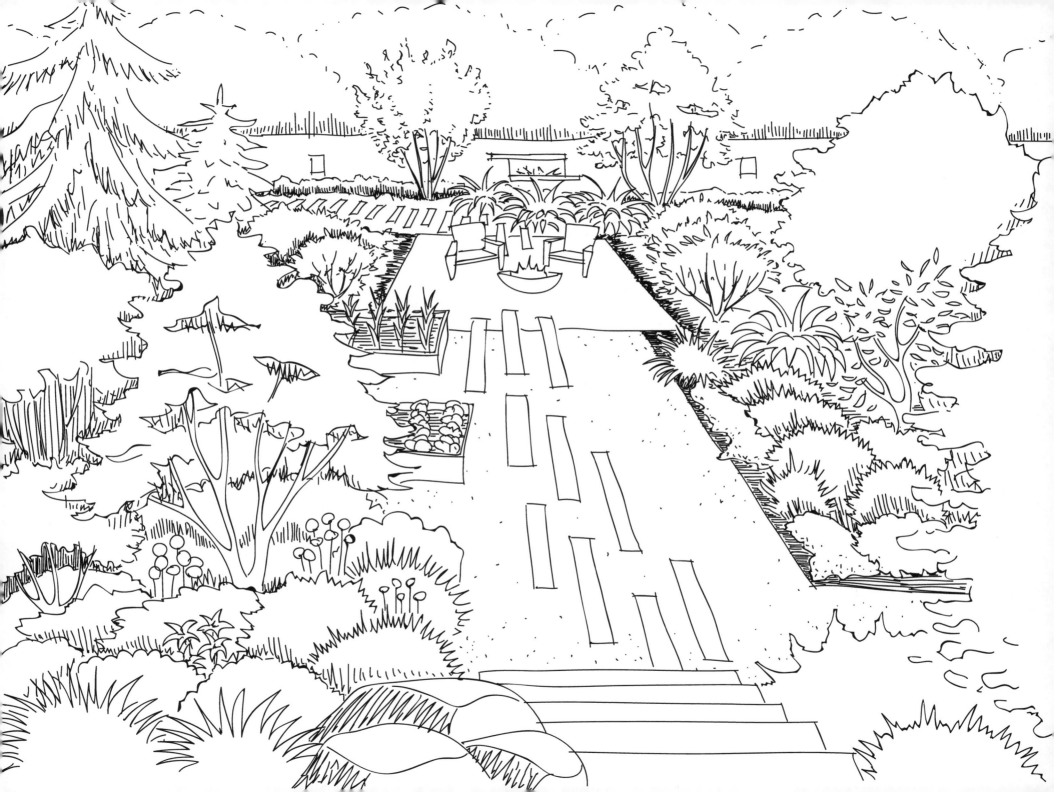

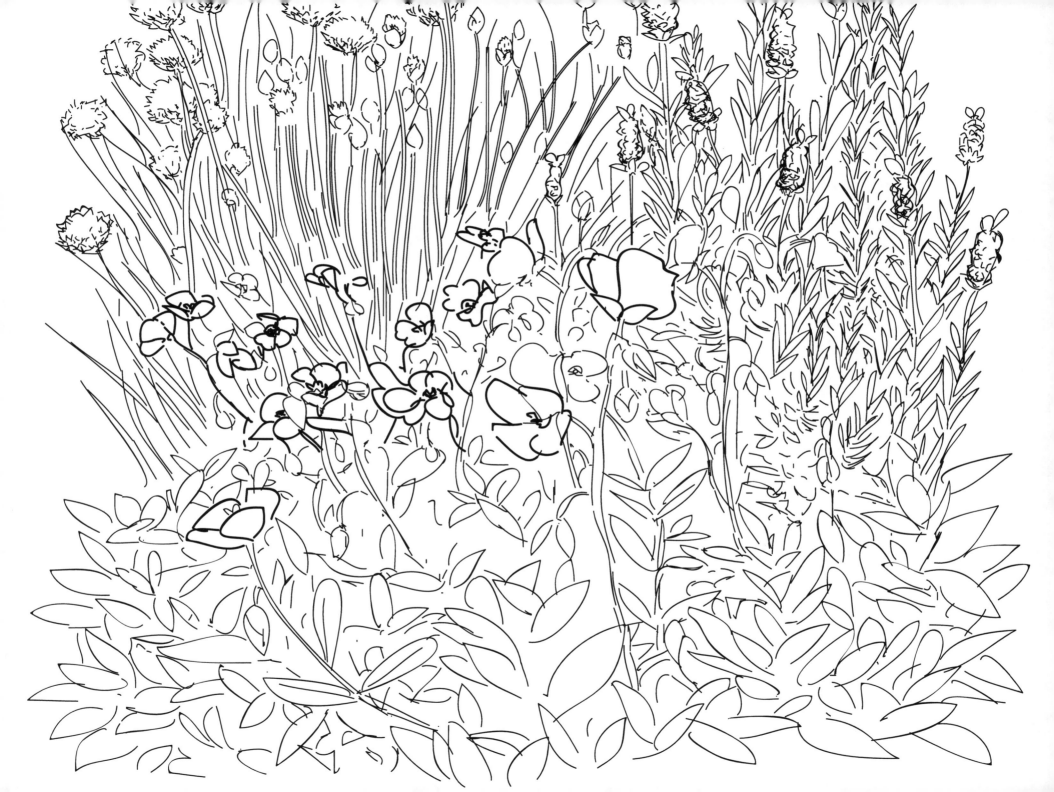

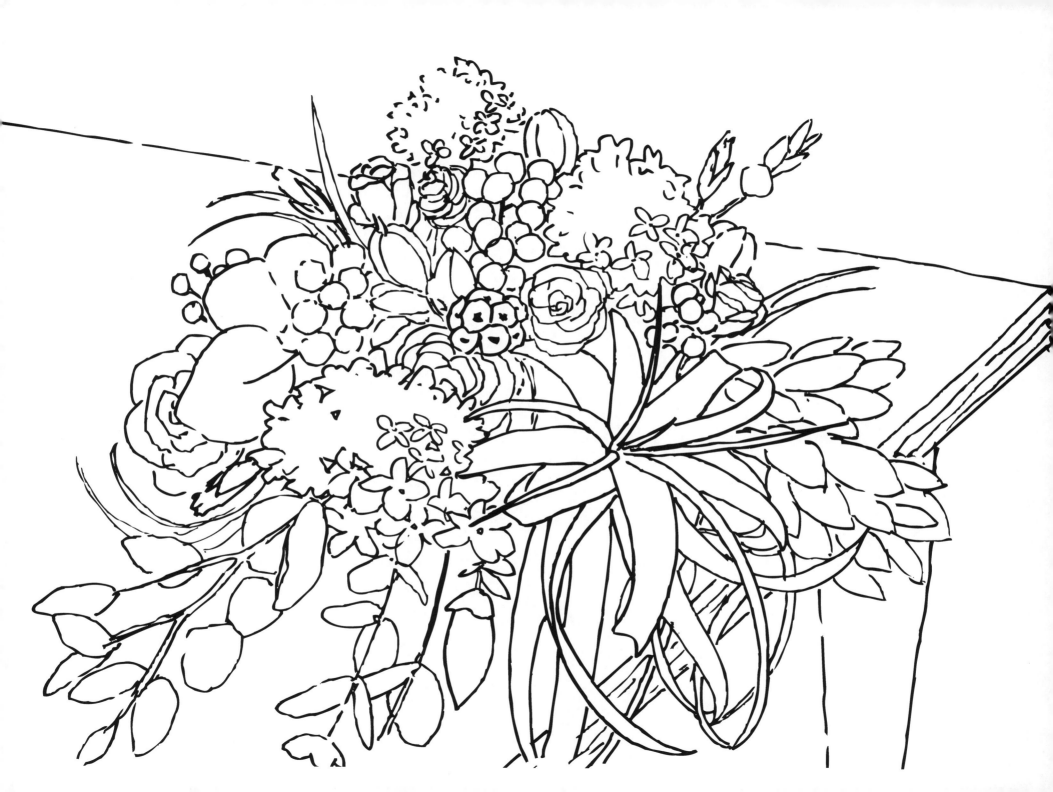

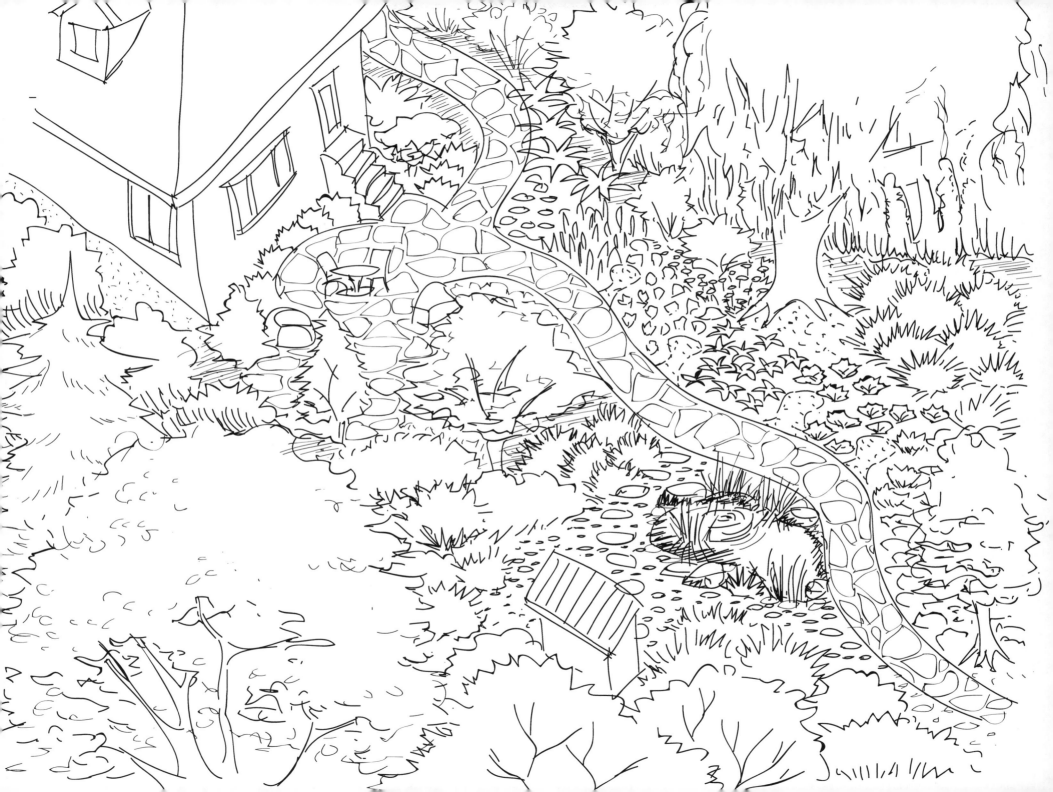

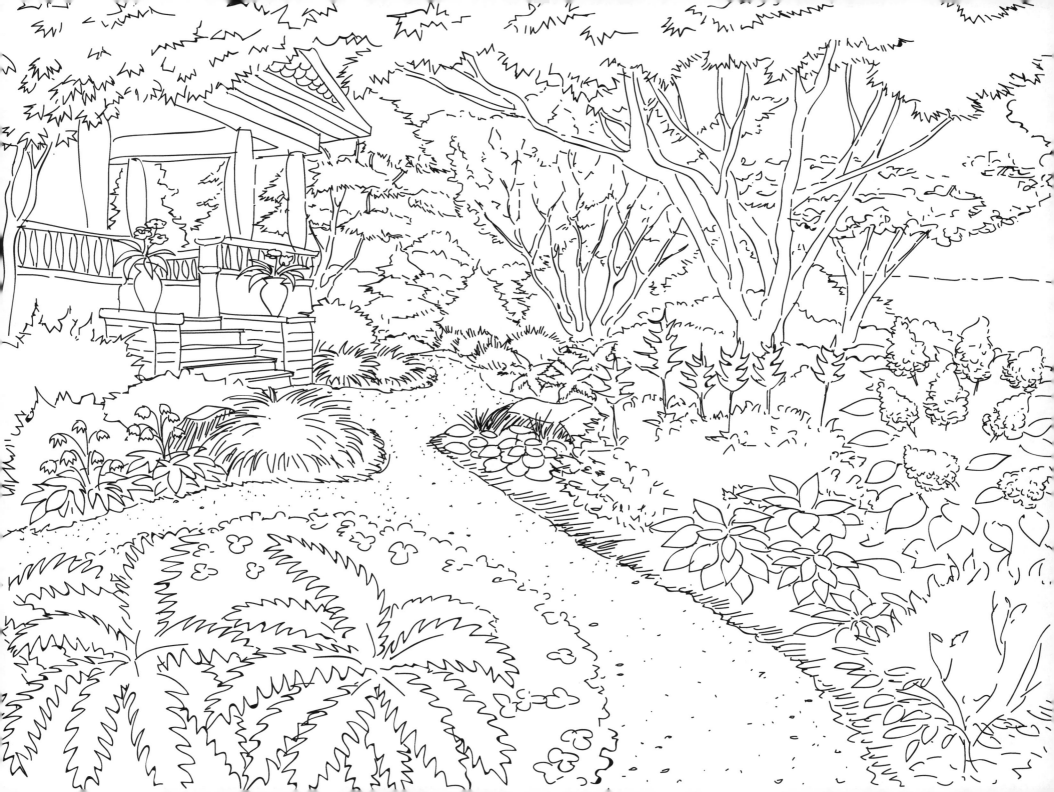

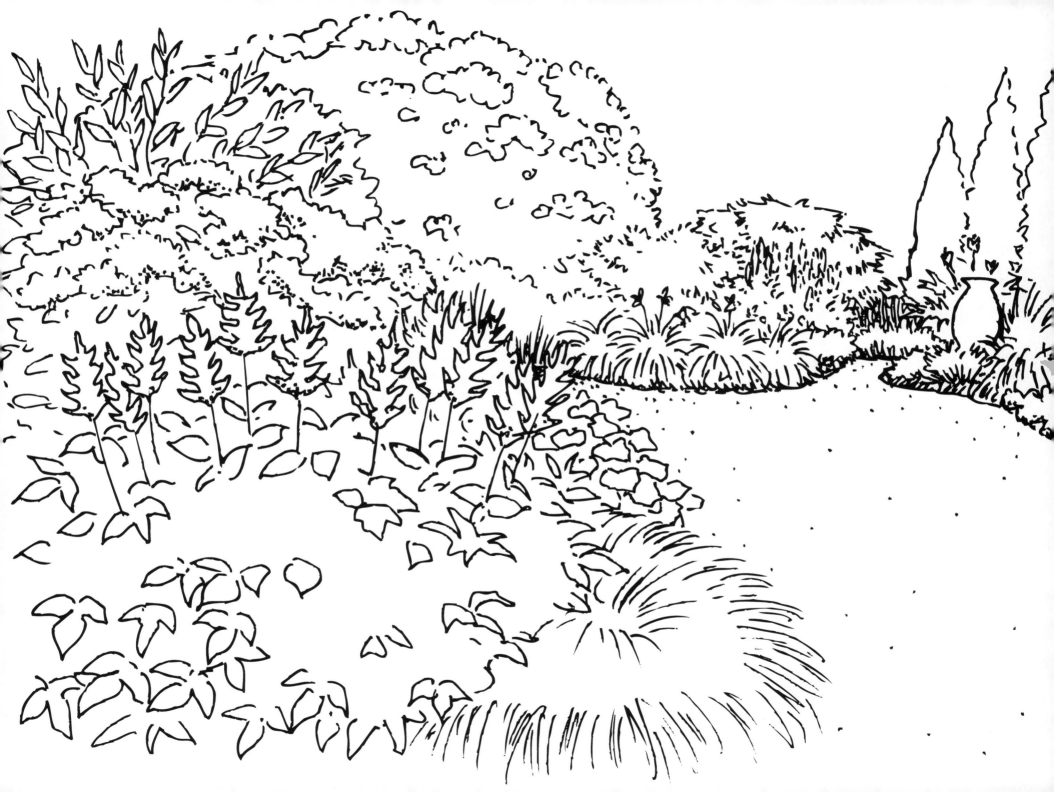

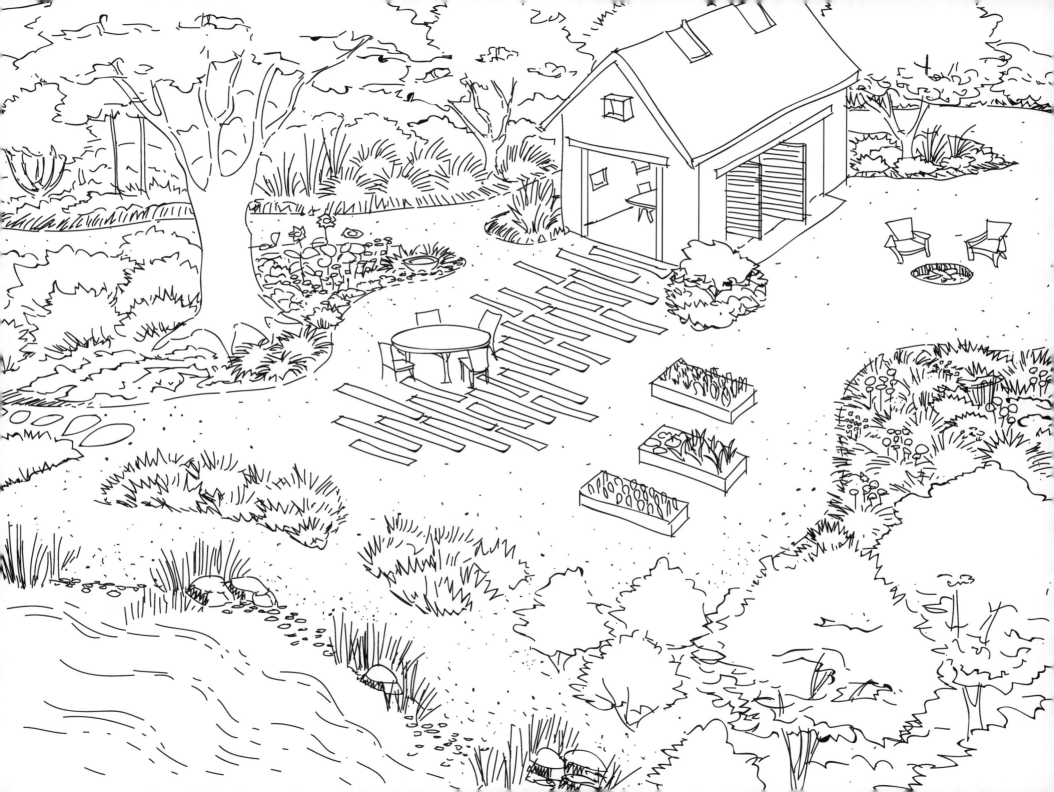

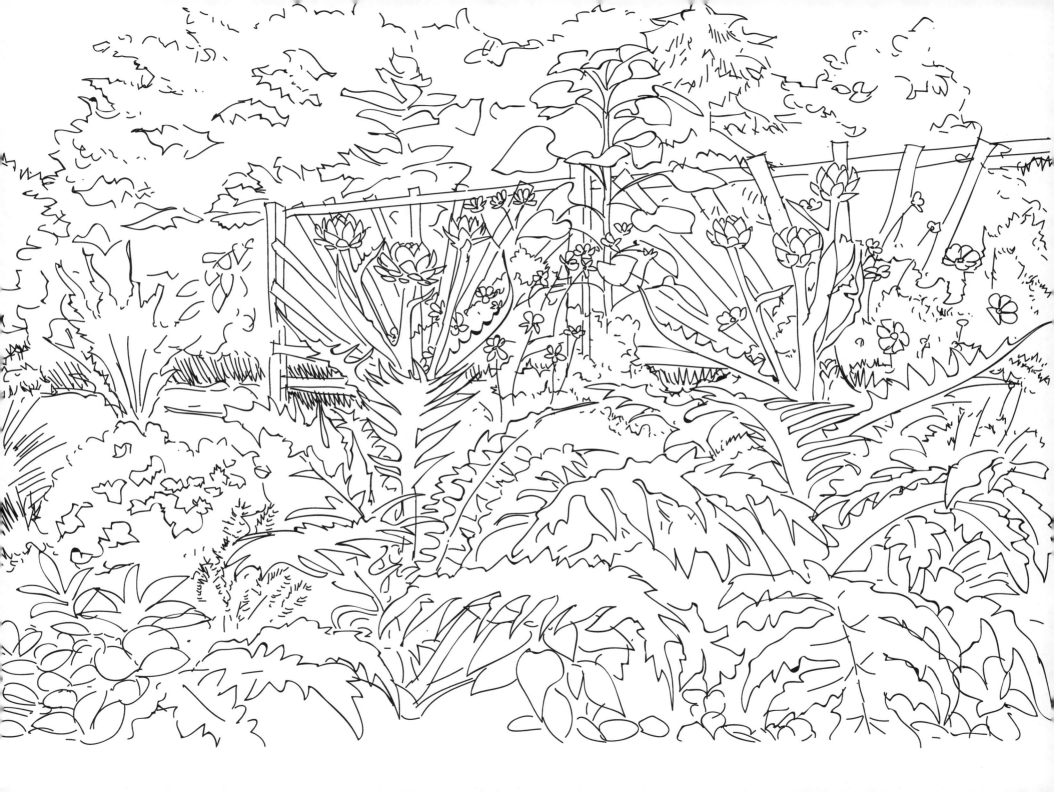

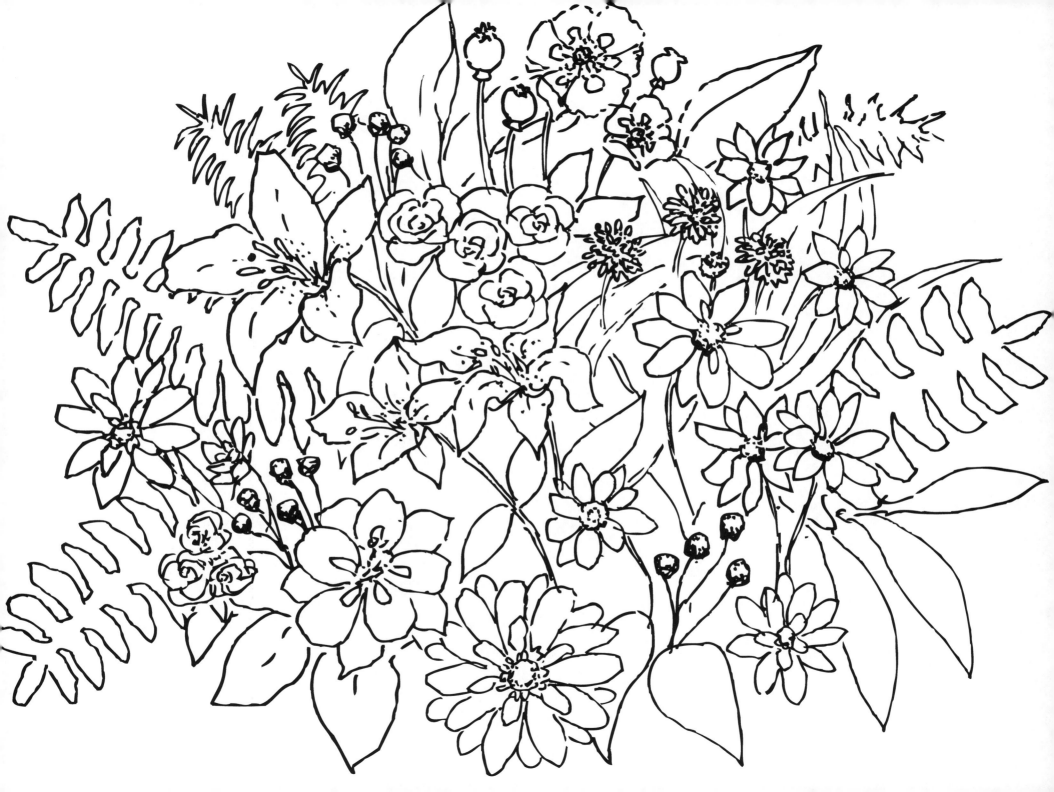

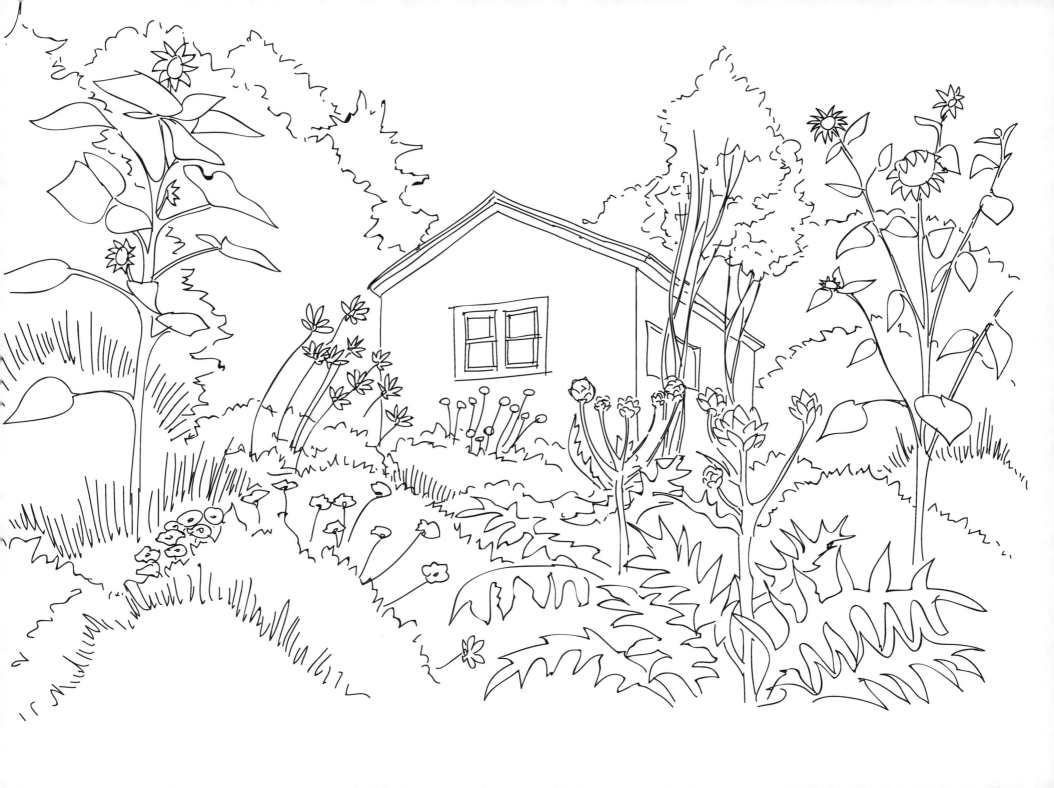

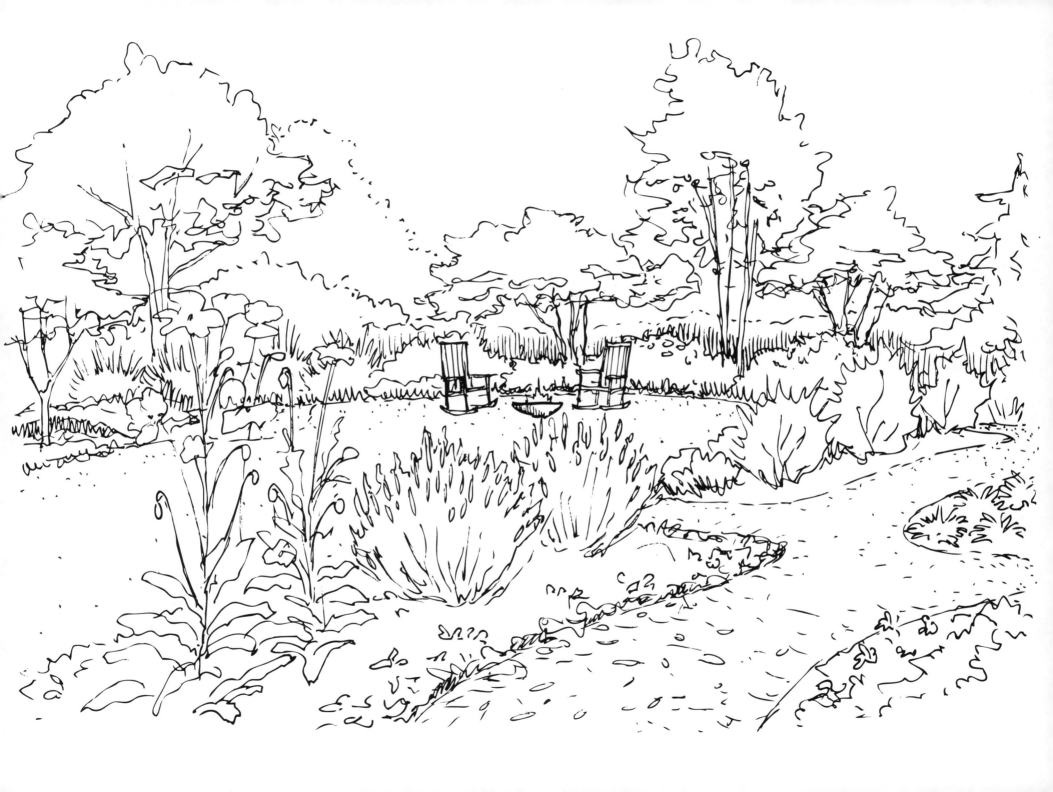

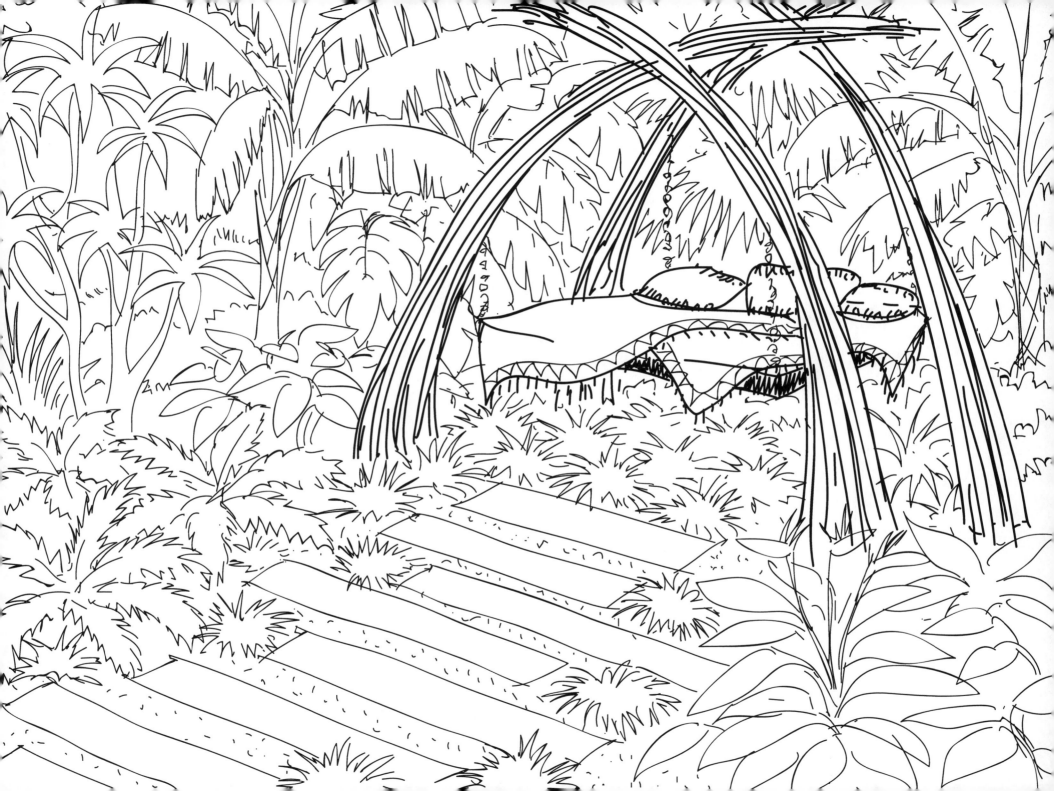

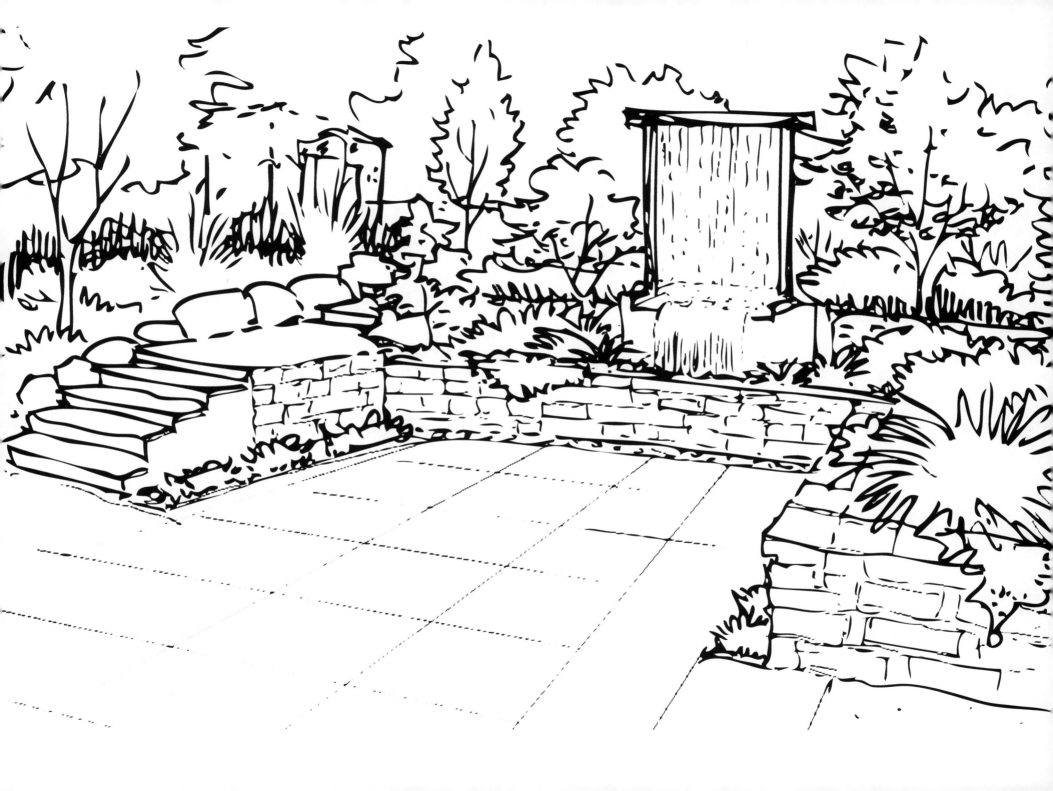

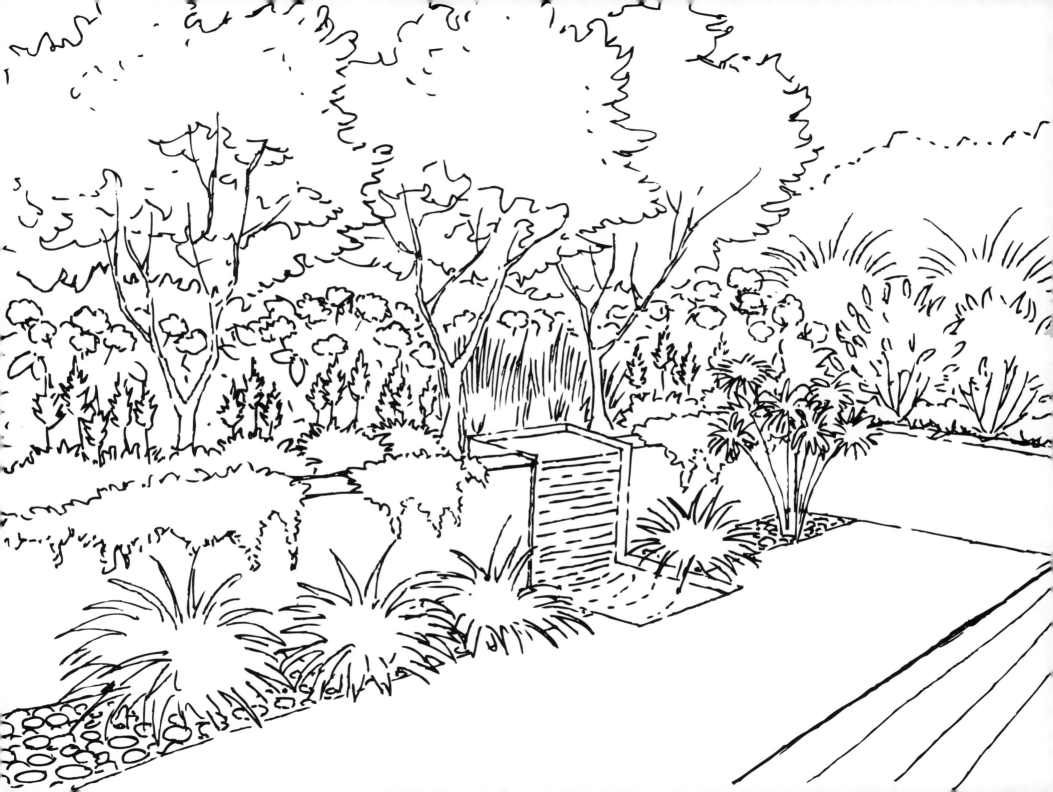

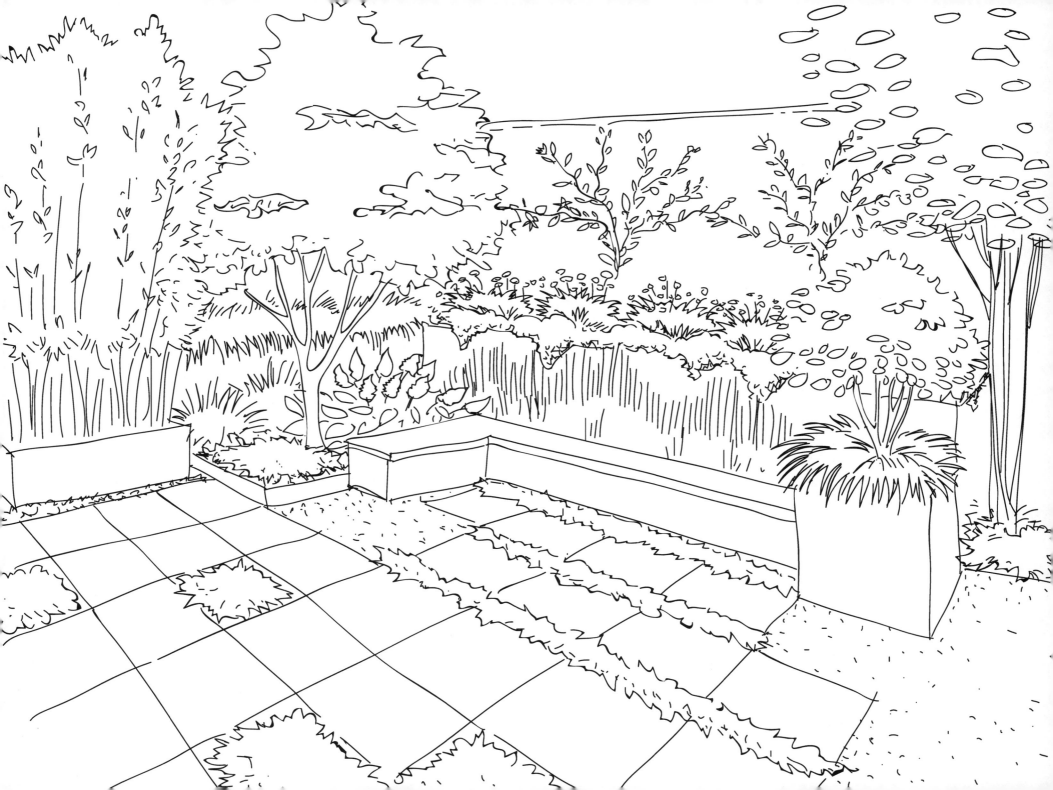

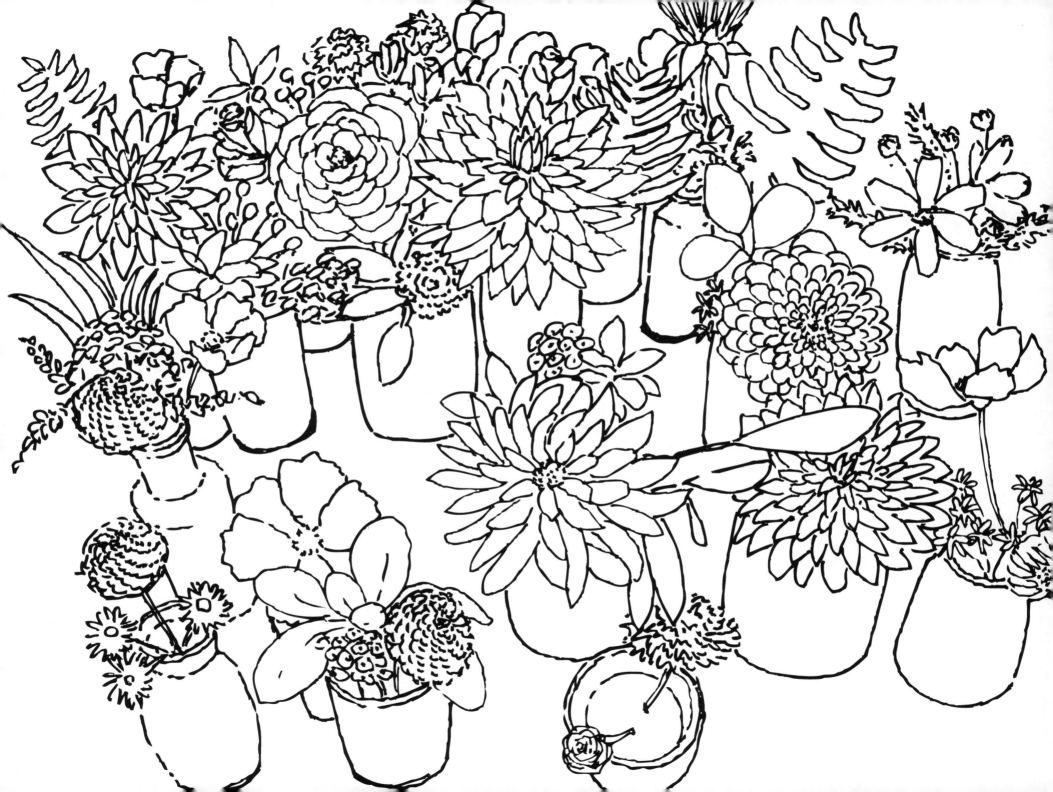

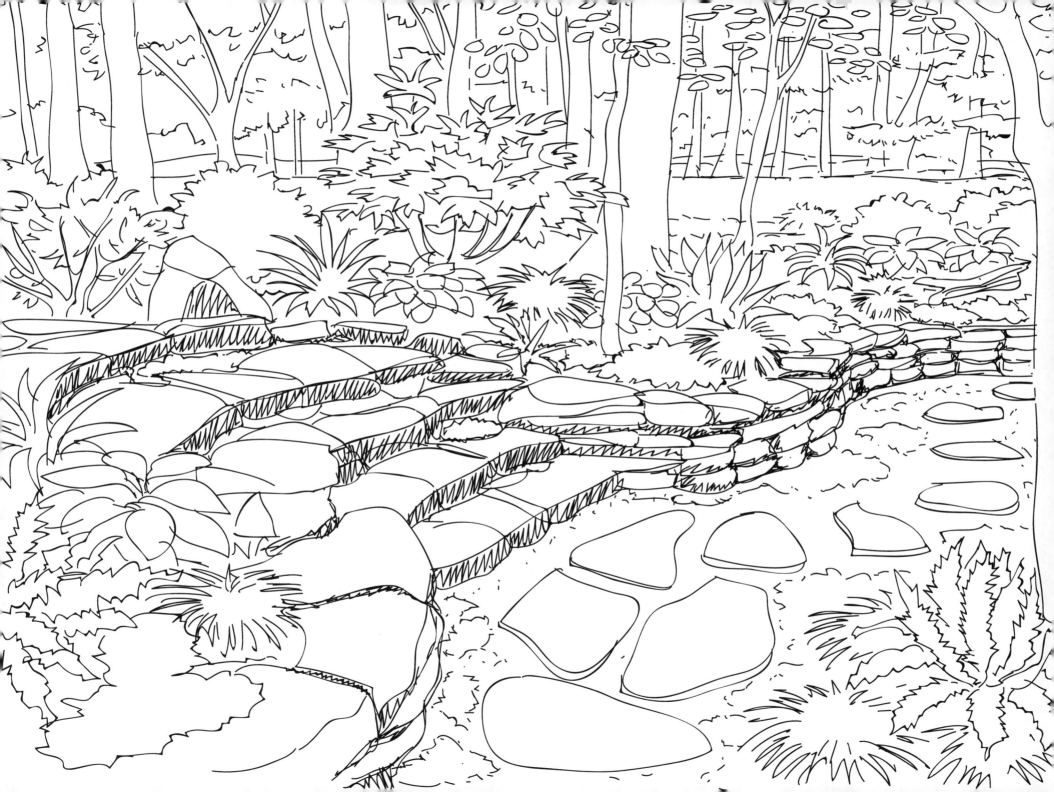

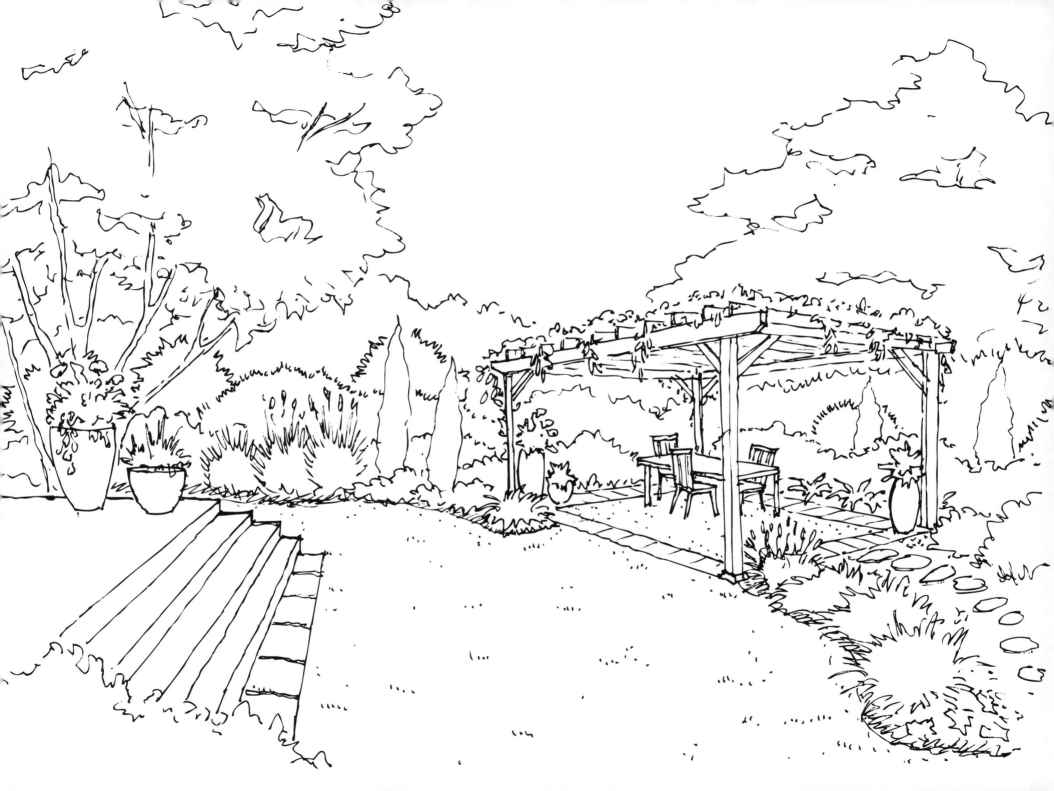

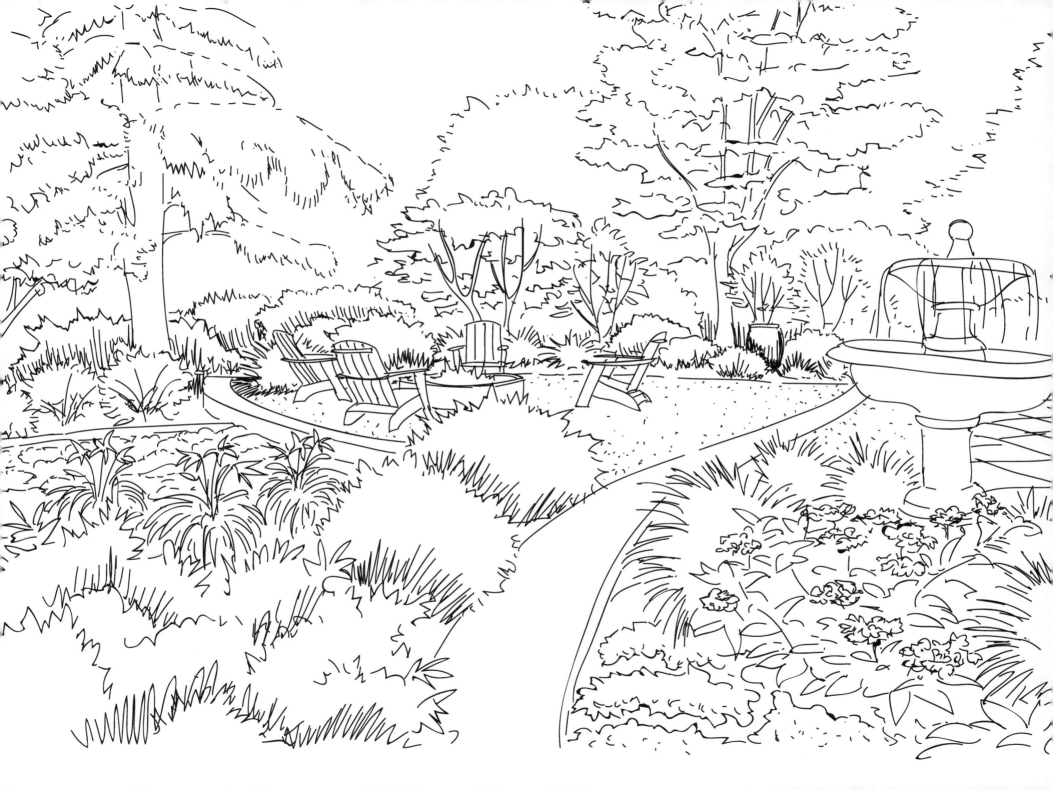

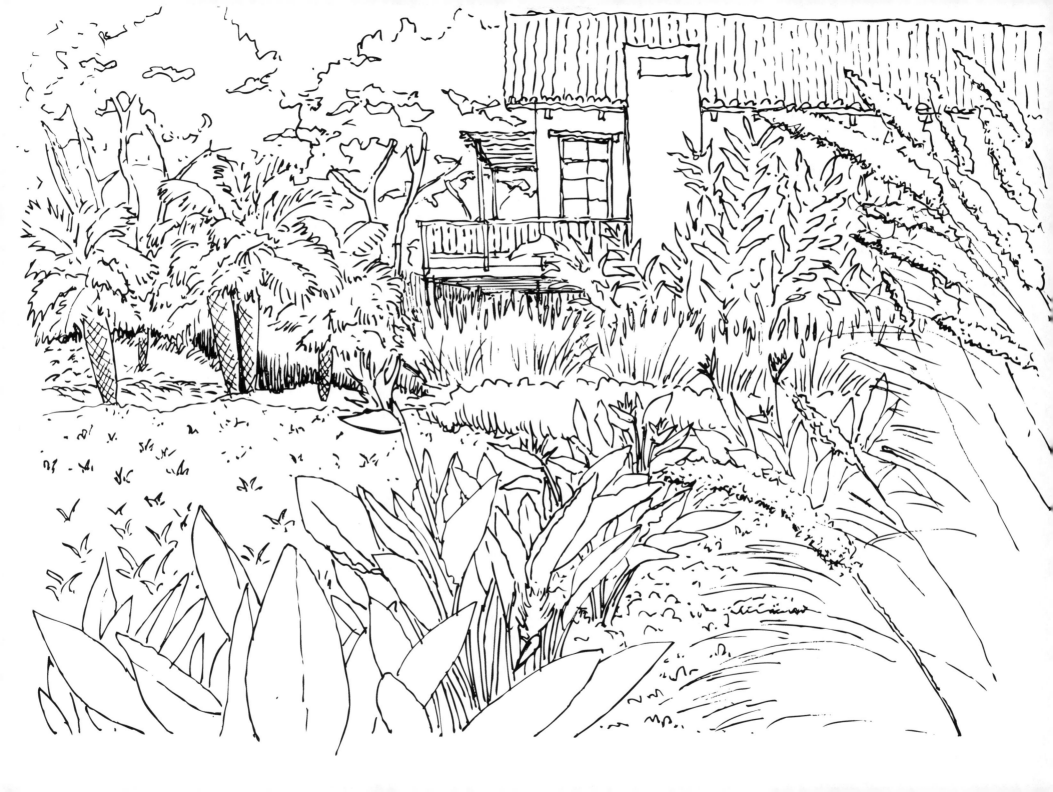

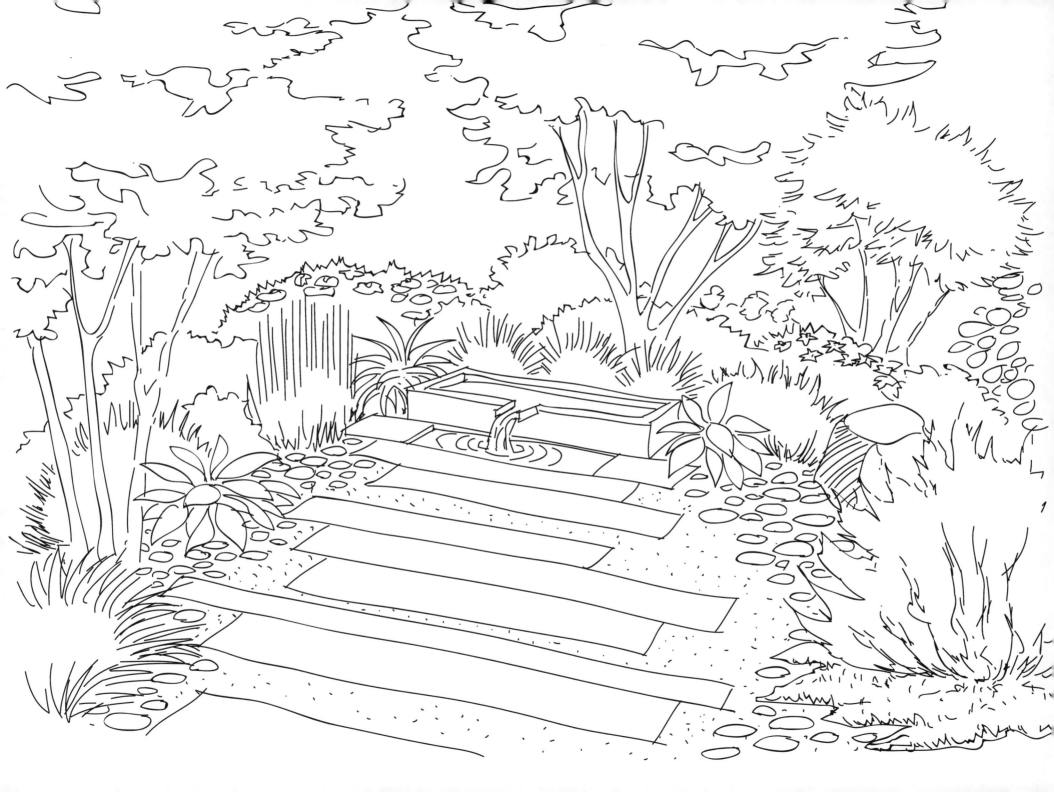

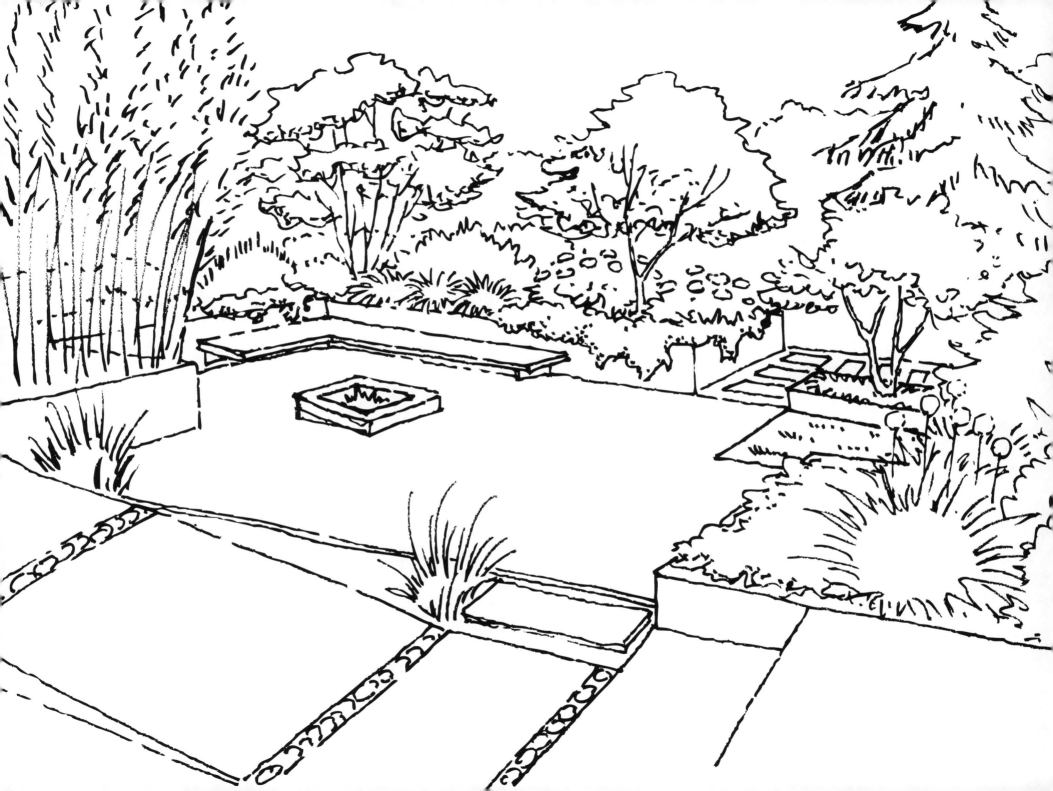

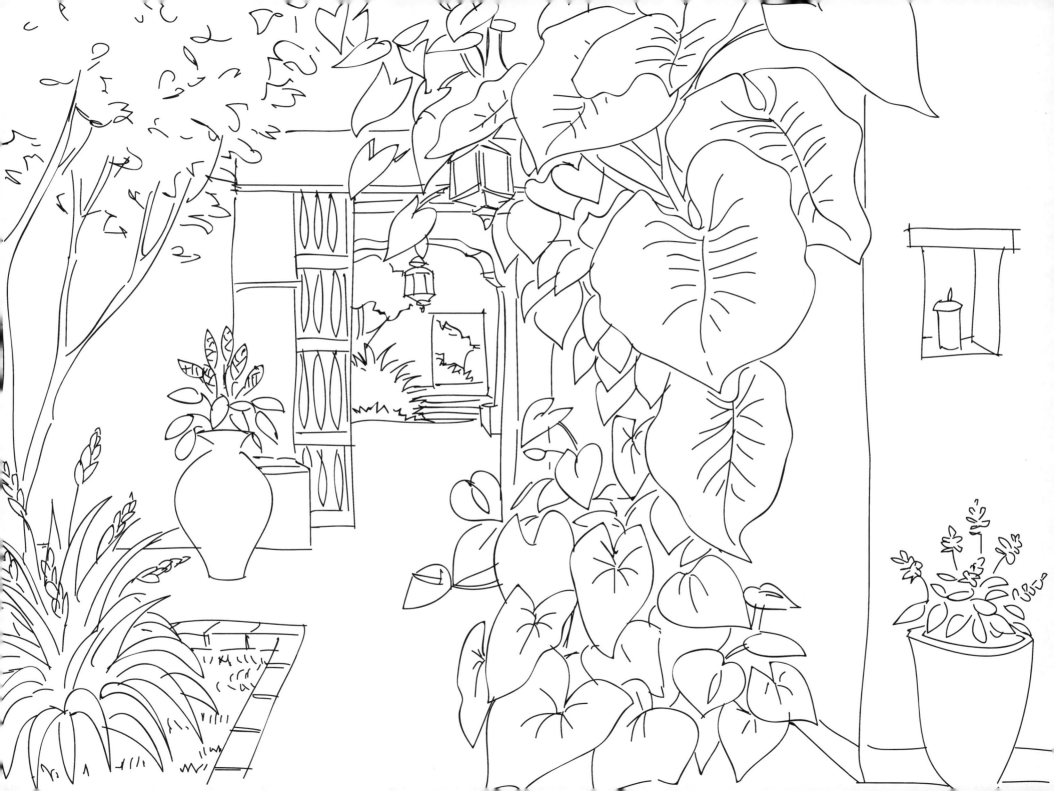

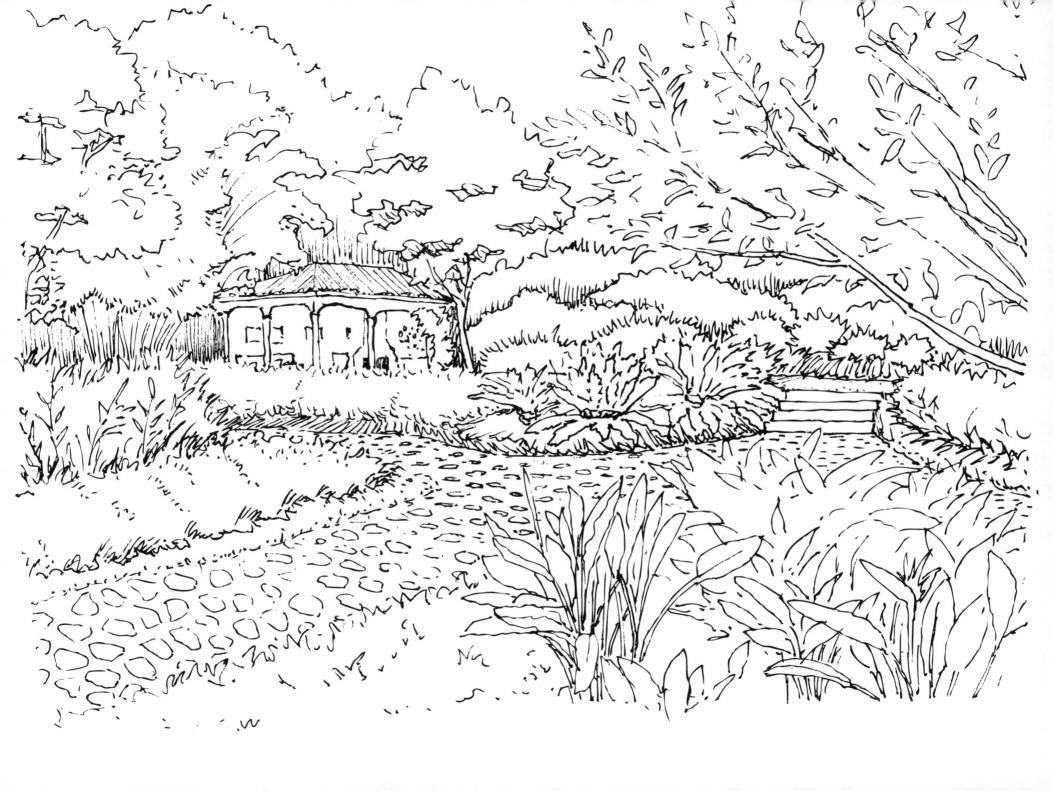

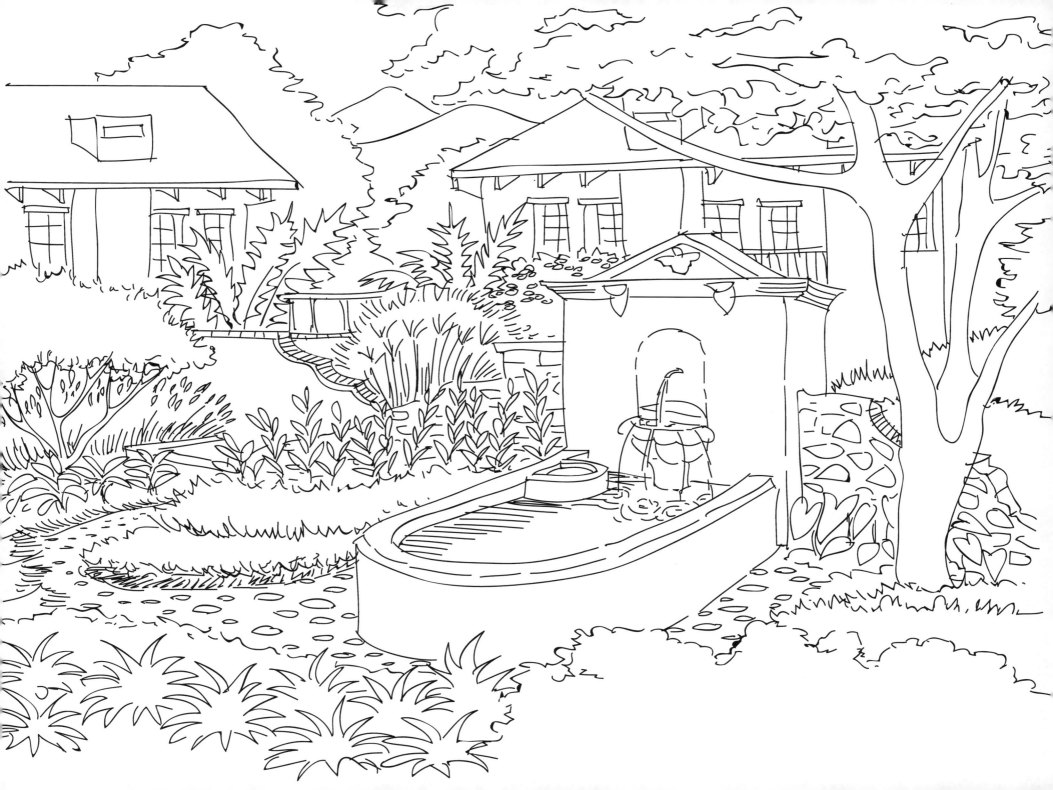

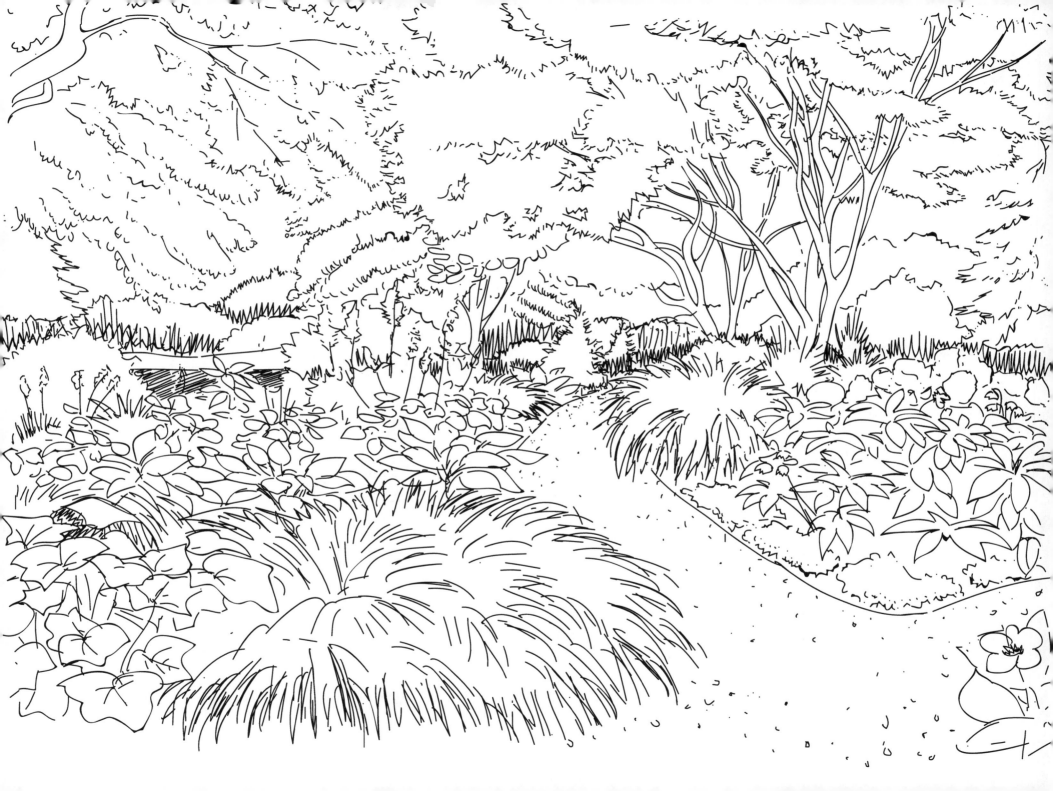

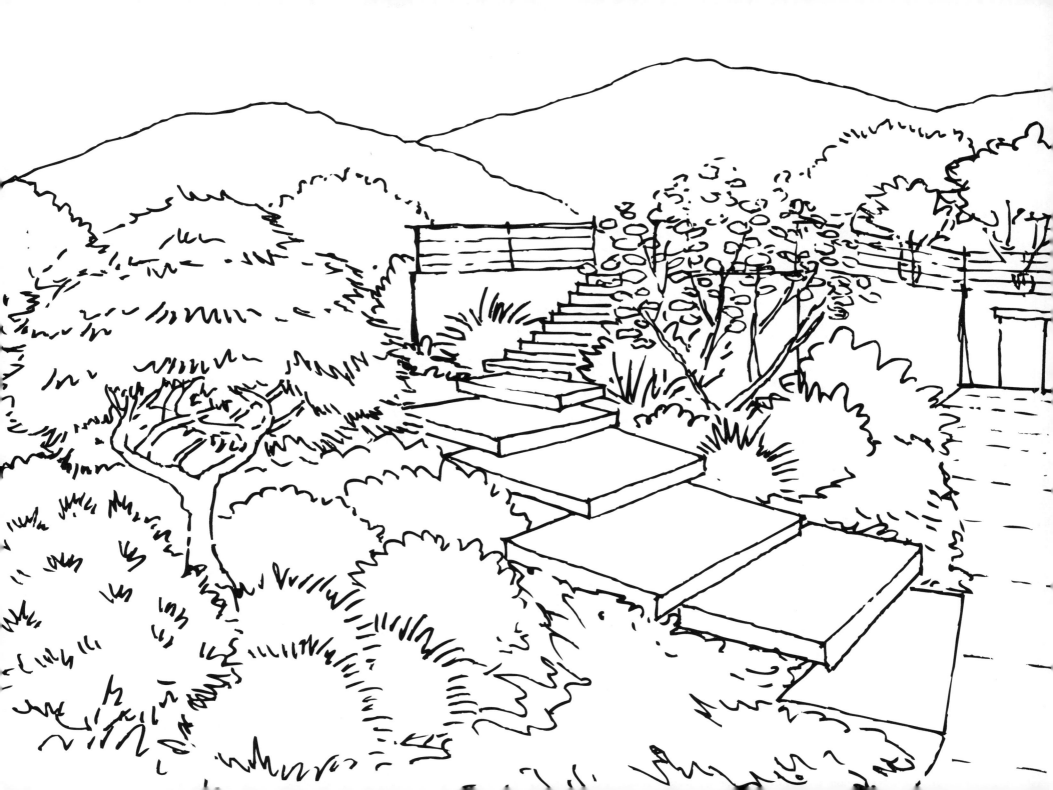

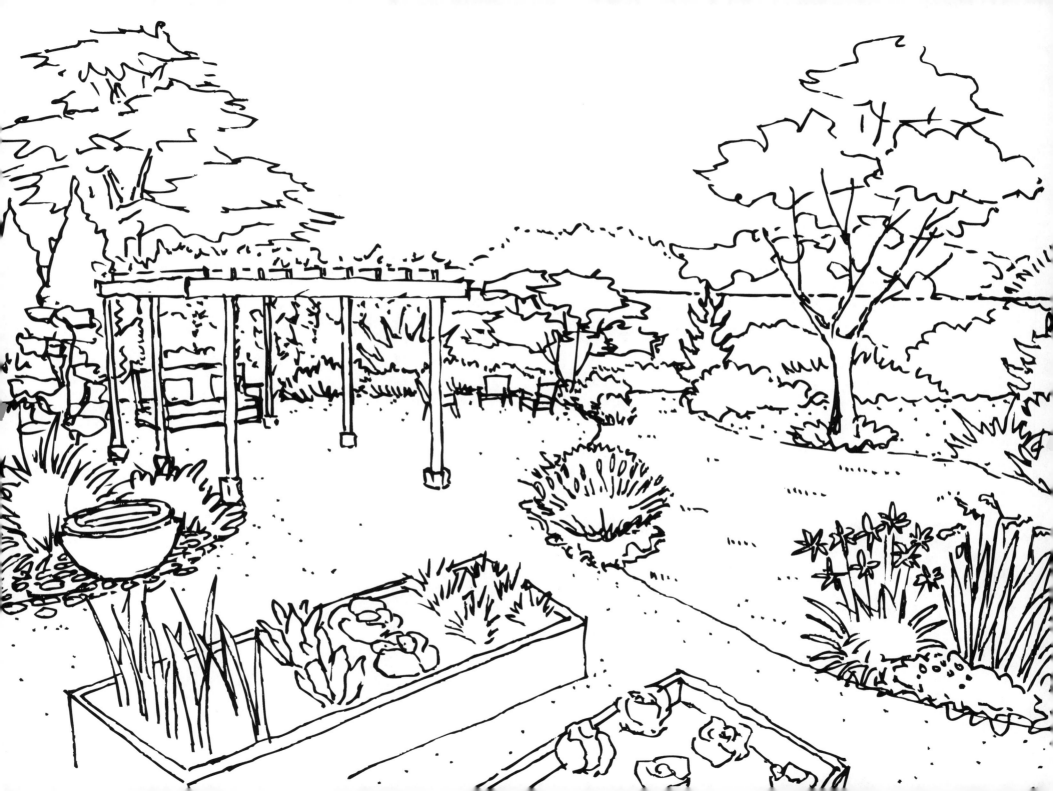

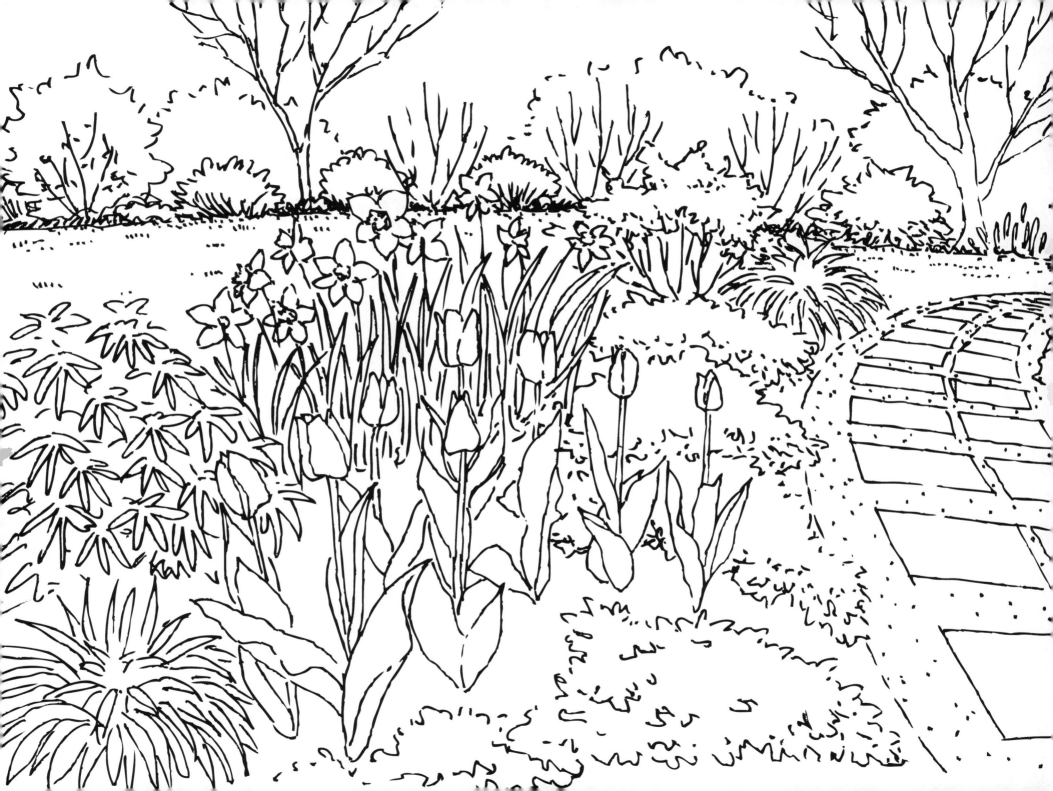

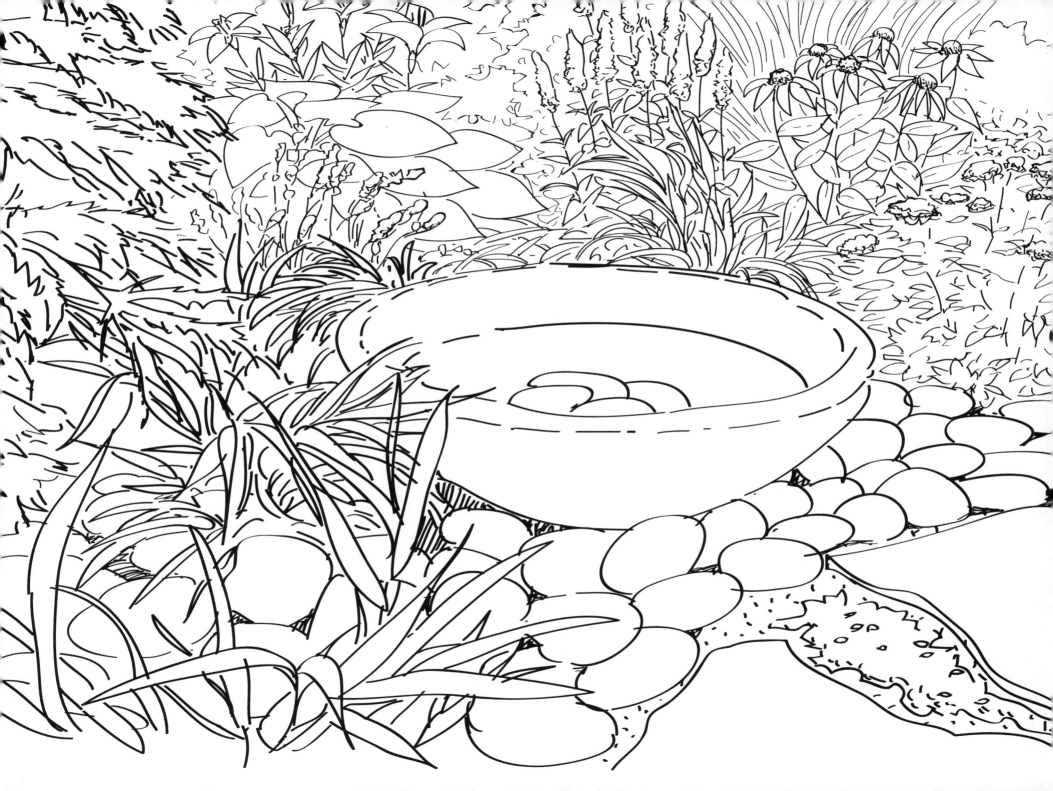

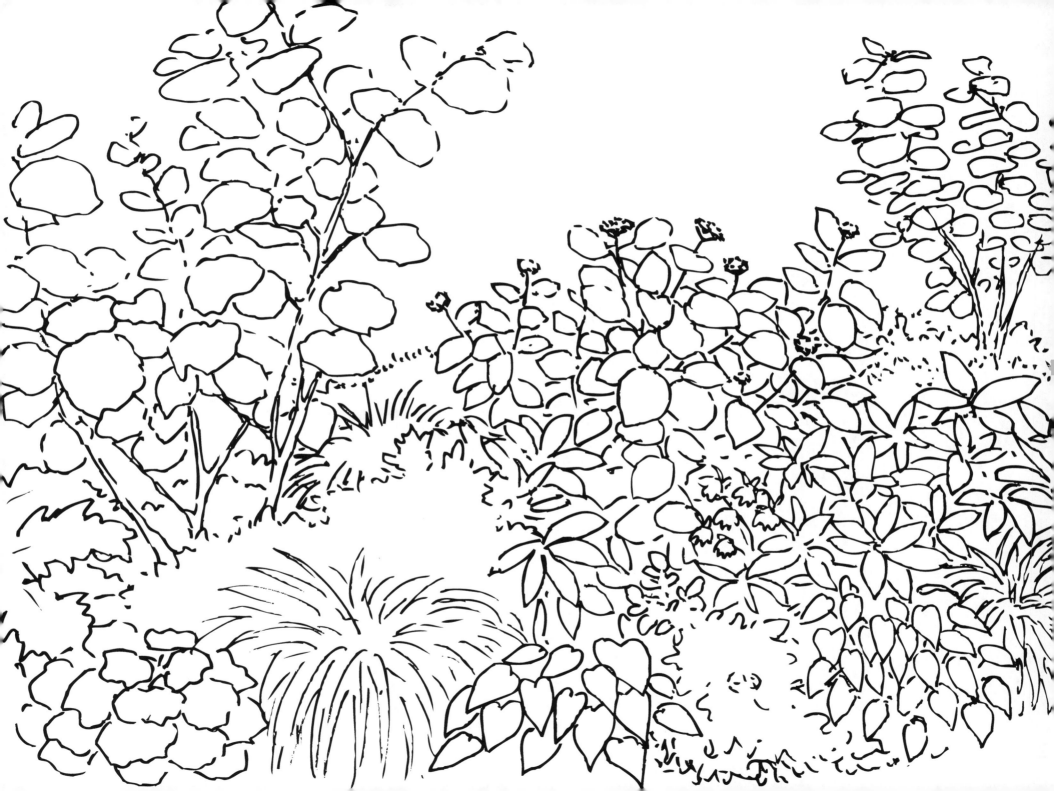

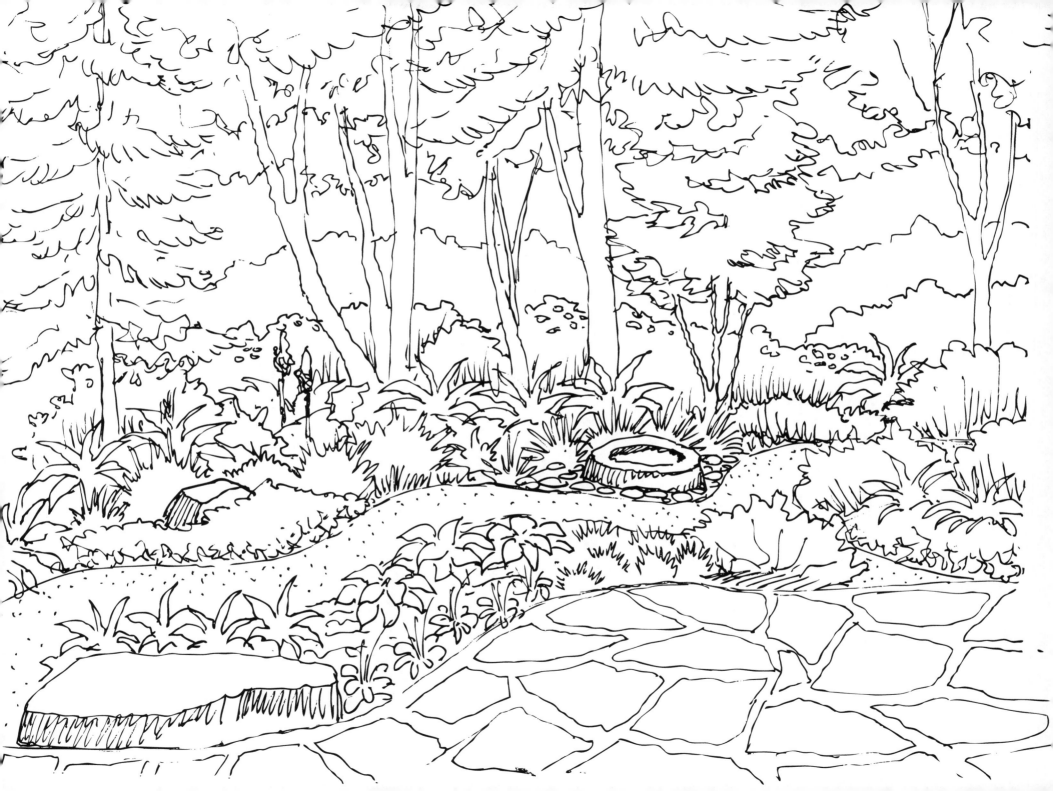

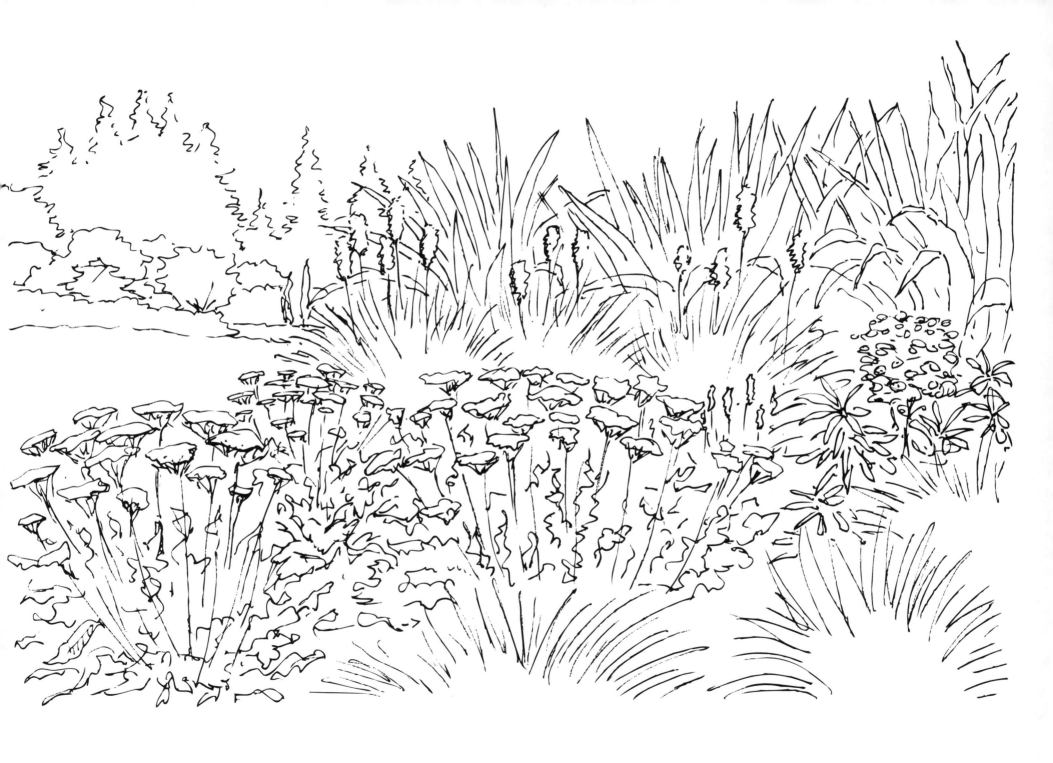

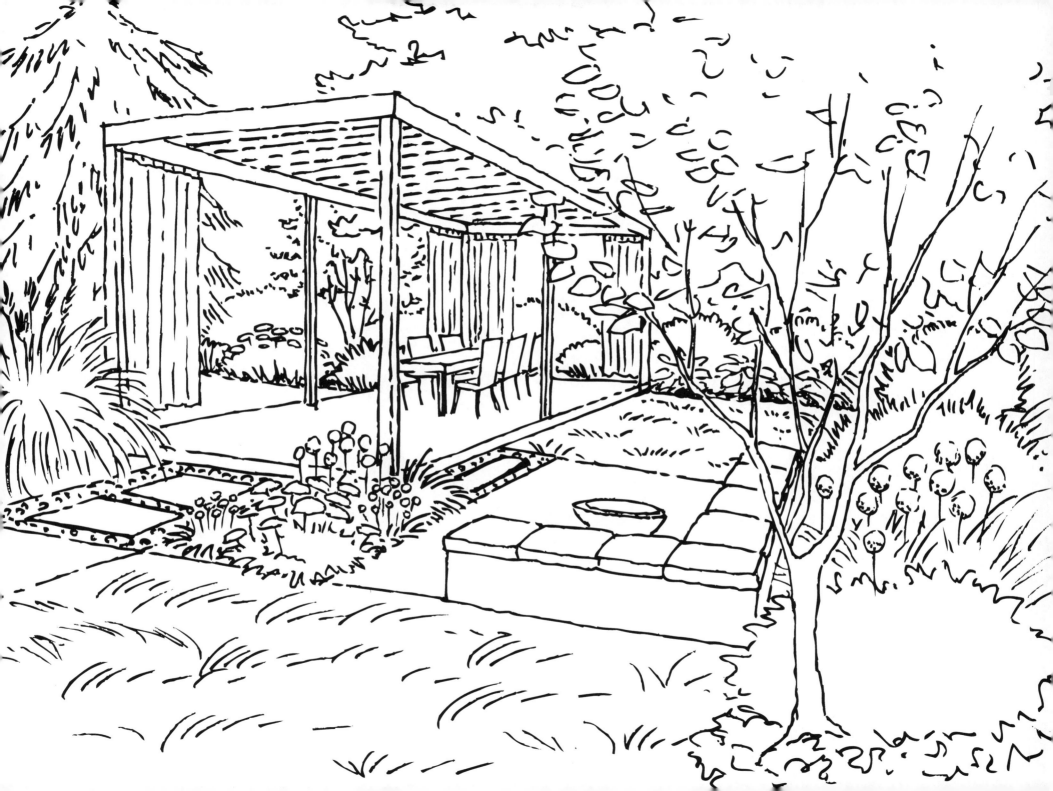

Made in the USA
Monee, IL
22 October 2022